Meat

The Taunton Press

ACADEMIA BARILLA
AMBASSADOR OF ITALIAN GASTRONOMY
THROUGHOUT THE WORLD

Academia Barilla is a global movement toward the protection, development and promotion of authentic regional Italian culture and cuisine.
With the concept of Food as Culture at our core, Academia Barilla offers a 360° view of Italy. Our comprehensive approach includes:

- a state-of-the-art culinary center in Parma, Italy;
- gourmet travel programs and hands-on cooking classes;
- the world's largest Italian gastronomic library and historic menu collection;
- a portfolio of premium artisan food products;
- global culinary certification programs;
- custom corporate services and training;
- team building activities;
- and a vast assortment of Italian cookbooks.

Thank you and we look forward to welcoming you in Italy soon!

CONTENTS

EDITED BY

ACADEMIA BARILLA

PHOTOGRAPHS

ALBERTO ROSSI

RECIPES BY

CHEF MARIO GRAZIA

CHEF LUCA ZANGA

TEXT BY

MARIAGRAZIA VILLA

ACADEMIA BARILLA EDITORIAL COORDINATION

CHATO MORANDI

ILARIA ROSSI

REBECCA PICKRELL

GRAPHIC DESIGN

PAOLA PIACCO

A MIGHTY PORTERHOUSE STEAK
AN INCH AND A HALF THICK, HOT AND
SPUTTERING FROM THE GRIDDLE; [...]
THE PRECIOUS JUICES OF THE MEAT
TRICKLING OUT AND JOINING THE GRAVY,
ARCHIPELAGOED WITH MUSHROOMS [...]

MARK TWAIN, *A TRAMP ABROAD*, 1878

MEAT

They may be called *secondi* in Italian, but meats and fish are not second in importance to anything. Quite the contrary. This is the course in the Italian meal that arrives just after the *primo* (or "first course," usually consisting of a pasta or soup dish), and represents the course with the most protein. The classic Italian *secondo*, nearly always accompanied by a side dish made from cooked or raw vegetables, is based on the use of meat or fish.

The choice among meats—including offal and lesser valued parts of the animal—and their culinary possibilities is truly extensive. Farm animals include capons, hens, chickens, turkeys and rabbits, which have white meat, and guinea fowl, geese, and ducks, with darker meat. Among these free-range animals, the chicken is still the star of many typical recipes from the *Bel Paese* (the "beautiful country," as Italians call their home). Until just a few decades ago, a roast chicken, served with potatoes and a nice garden salad, was the symbolic Sunday lunch for many Italians.

Meat from cattle includes beef and veal, sourced from animals at different ages. Veal meat, especially popular in Italian cuisine, is white and has a smooth and delicate flavor, whereas beef is red, with a more decisive taste. And pork, of course, comes from the pig; its meat has been used for centuries, from north to south along the peninsula, in preparing delicious and highly prized main-course meals, as well as excellent sausages. (As an old saying goes, "Every part of the pig is used but the squeal!")

Goat, sheep, and game meats are decisively stronger in flavor, and closer to nature. Among these, lamb and suckling kid goats are the favorites, because of their less intense flavor. In regions of central Italy, they are the highlights of the Easter banquet. Game meat—so delicious that, since the beginning of the last century, it has taken pride of place on the banquet tables of nobles—can include venison, hare, wild boar, woodcock, pheasant, duck and partridge.

With its mission of preserving and promoting Italian cuisine, Academia Barilla, the international center dedicated to the preservation and promotion of Italian gastronomy, has selected 40 excellent recipes for meat-based main-course dishes from the Italian tradition. Some of the dishes are very simple and can be prepared in less than an hour, like the grilled lamb ribs, the Veal Scaloppine alla Pizzaiola (veal in a zesty tomato sauce), or the potato and veal meatballs, whereas others are a bit more elaborate, requiring greater care and attention in the execution. For the veal breast, for example, it is very important to perfectly close the "pocket" of veal after stuffing, otherwise it might break as it cooks and spill out all the stuffing. But from the most straightforward to the most complex, all of these succulent and hearty main course dishes are capable of conversing with the great products of Italian tradition, from the great wines to balsamic vinegar of Modena, from mushrooms to truffles, from cheeses to cured meats.

The Tuscan-Style Roast Loin of Pork, for example, is prepared with a cut of pork (*arista*) which takes its name, according to legend, from an exclamation made by the Greek Cardinal Basilios Bessarion. After tasting this delicious roast during a banquet held in Florence in 143 on the occasion of the ecumenical council of the Greek and Roman Churches, he is said to have exclaimed "Aristos, aristos!" meaning, "The best, the best!" Obviously, this pleased the Florentines.

The Roman Oxtail Stew was born in the early twentieth century in the restaurants that grew up around the capital's slaughterhouses, where cooks collected the unsaleable parts of the cow, such as, the tail. And did you know that there are two types of the Milanese cutlet (the Costoletta alla Milanese, more frequently called the Cotoletta alla Milanese)? One type is "with the bone" (con l'osso) retaining the rib, which can be used a bit like a handle, and requires pounding the meat only a little bit. The other, "elephant-ear style" (a orecchia d'elefante), a crunchier version with a stronger flavor of the fried breading, has the bone eliminated, and the meat must be pounded until it becomes a broad, deliciously thin slice.

The dishes you will discover here are prepared by way of many cooking methods; and they each have a story to reveal, a variation to suggest.

ROAST VEAL IN MILK

Preparation time: 20 minutes   Cooking time: 1 hour   Difficulty: easy

4 SERVINGS

1 3/4 lbs. (800 g) **veal rump roast**
1 3/4 oz. (50 g) **Parma ham**, *finely chopped*
3 1/2 tbsp. (50 g) **unsalted butter**
4 cups (1 l) **milk**
1 3/4 oz. (50 g) **all-purpose flour**, *or about 1/2 cup*
Salt and pepper *to taste*

Warm the butter in a pot over medium heat and sauté the ham. Use three-quarters of the flour to coat the veal, season with salt and pepper, and fry gently, browning on all sides. Add some of the milk, reduce heat to low and leave to cook, adding more milk and basting during cooking so that the meat is kept moist. When the veal is fork-tender, in about 45 minutes, add the remaining flour, stir and simmer until sauce thickens. Slice veal and serve it in the sauce obtained from the cooking juices.

VEAL BOCCONCINI
WITH POTATOES AND PEAS

Preparation time: 30 minutes   Cooking time: 1 1/2 hours   Difficulty: easy

4 SERVINGS

1 1/3 lbs. (600 g) **veal**, *cut into bite-size pieces*
1 oz. (25 g) **leek**, *sliced*
3 1/2 oz. (100 g) **onion**, *chopped*
1 oz. (30 g) **celery**, *chopped*
1 1/2 tbsp. (20 g) **unsalted butter**
4 cups (1 l) **vegetable or beef broth**
7 oz. (200 g) **potatoes**, *peeled and cut into sticks*
4 oz. (100 g) **peas**
1/3 cup plus 1 1/2 tbsp. (100 ml) **white wine**
3 1/2 tbsp. (50 ml) **extra-virgin olive oil**
1/3 cup plus 1 1/2 tbsp. (100 ml) **milk**
Salt and pepper *to taste*

Heat the butter and oil in a skillet and brown the leek, onion and celery. Add the veal and brown all together.

Season with salt and pepper, and add the white wine. Let the wine evaporate, and gradually moisten with the broth. Cook for about 1 hour.

Blanch the potatoes for 5 minutes in boiling salted water, drain, and add to the veal mixture.

Add the peas and continue cooking for about 15 minutes. Lastly, add the milk, and reduce the sauce to a desired consistency. Serve.

BEEF BRAISED IN BAROLO WINE

Preparation time: 30 minutes   Marinating time: 12 hours
Cooking time: 3 hours   Difficulty: high

4 SERVINGS

3 1/3 lbs. (1.5 kg) **beef shoulder**
1 bottle **Barolo wine** (or any full-
   bodied red wine)
3 1/2 tbsp. (50 ml) **extra-virgin olive oil**
2 cloves **garlic**, chopped
1 **onion**, diced
1 large **carrot**, diced
2 stalks **celery**, diced

1 **sprig fresh rosemary**
1 **bunch fresh sage**
1 **fresh bay leaf**
1 **clove**
1 **stick cinnamon**
3-4 **peppercorns**
Salt to taste

Tie the beef shoulder with kitchen twine and put it in a bowl with the spices,
herbs and vegetables. Cover with the wine and marinate in the refrigerator for
12 hours. Remove the meat from the marinade and pat it dry. Strain the
vegetables and reserve the marinade.
Heat the oil in a pot and brown the meat all over. Add the vegetables and
continue to cook, then pour in the marinade liquid to cover, add salt and cover
the pan. Cook beef over low heat for about 3 hours, until it is tender. When
cooked, remove it from the pot and let it rest on a cutting board. Meanwhile,
put the sauce through a vegetable mill (or blend in a food processor), filter it in a
sieve and, if too thin, reduce to desired consistency. Cut the meat into thick
slices and immerse in the sauce for a while to acquire flavor before serving.

STUFFED VEAL BREAST

Preparation time: 1 hour   Cooking time: 2 hours   Difficulty: high

4 SERVINGS

1 lb. 10 oz. (750 g) **veal breast** (ask your butcher to cut a pocket at one end)
3 1/2 oz. (100 g) **ground veal**
1 3/4 oz. (50 g) **dried mushrooms**, such as porcini
3 1/2 oz. (100 g) **pine nuts**, or about 2/3 cup
1 3/4 oz. (50 g) **Parmigiano-Reggiano cheese**, grated, or about 1/2 cup
1 3/4 oz. (50 g) **peas**
3 large **eggs**
1 clove **garlic**, chopped
Fresh marjoram to taste
Grated **nutmeg** to taste
Salt and pepper to taste

Boil the eggs for about 6 minutes, let them cool and then shell them. Soak the dried mushrooms in lukewarm water for at least one hour and then squeeze to remove excess moisture and chop them. Parboil the peas in salted water for 2 minutes and let them cool.

Put the ground veal in a large bowl with the cheese, garlic, mushrooms and pine nuts; season with salt, pepper, nutmeg and marjoram. Combine well. Gently incorporate the peas, and spoon this mixture into the veal breast along with the whole hard-cooked eggs. Close the veal pocket with a kitchen needle. Wrap the breast in cheesecloth and secure it with kitchen twine. Place it in a large pot and cover with cold water. Bring the water to a boil, reduce the heat to low and simmer until tender, about 2 hours. Let the veal cool in the cooking water, and once it has cooled, remove the cloth, slice the meat and serve.

ROMAN OXTAIL STEW

Preparation time: 20 minutes   Cooking time: 4 hours   Difficulty: medium

4 SERVINGS

2 1/4 lbs. (1 kg) **oxtail**, *cut into pieces*
1 **onion**, *chopped*
1 **carrot**, *chopped*
1 stalk **celery**, *chopped*
3/4 cup plus 1 1/2 tbsp. (200 ml) **dry white wine**
1 cup (200 g) **crushed tomatoes**
5 tsp. (25 ml) **extra-virgin olive oil**
1 tsp. (5 g) **fresh parsley**, *chopped*
Crushed red pepper flakes *to taste*
Salt and pepper *to taste*

Parboil the oxtail in unsalted water for 5 minutes. Drain the meat.
Heat the oil in a pot over moderate heat until shimmering. Brown the onion,
parsley and carrot, with a little crushed red pepper.
Add the meat and a little salt and pepper and cook until the meat beings to
change color. When it has acquired a uniform golden color, add the wine and
cook until it has evaporated. Add the tomatoes and enough water to cover the
meat completely. Simmer over low heat, covered, for 4 hours, adding water
whenever the stew becomes too dry.
Add the celery to the pot after about 3 3/4 hours (or about 15 minutes before
the meat is tender).

SARDINIAN BEEF ROLLS

Preparation time: 20 minutes   *Cooking time: 10 minutes*   *Difficulty: easy*

4 SERVINGS

8 **slices beef round steak**
1 3/4 oz. (50 g) **lard or bacon**, *finely chopped*
2 cloves **garlic**, *finely chopped*
1 **sprig fresh parsley**, *finely chopped*
4 tsp. (20 ml) **extra-virgin olive oil**
4 tsp. (20 ml) **white wine**
1/2 cup (100 ml) **beef broth**
Salt and pepper *to taste*

Using a meat mallet, gently pound out the slices of beef until 1/10 inch (3 mm) thin. Season with salt and pepper. Mix together the garlic, parsley and lard, and spread a little on each slice of meat. Roll up each slice of meat, forming a cylinder, and use a toothpick or kitchen string to secure it. Heat the oil in a skillet and brown the meat on all sides. Once nicely browned, add the broth and simmer, covered, over very low heat until tender. As the meat begins to feel tender, add the white wine. Cook uncovered for another few minutes, remove the toothpicks or string and serve.

MILANESE-STYLE CUTLETS

Preparation time: 20 minutes   *Cooking time: 8 minutes*   *Difficulty: easy*

4 SERVINGS

4 **veal cutlets**, *each weighing approximately 7 oz. (200 g), or 4 bone-in veal chops*
2 large **eggs**
3 1/2 oz. (100 g) **dried breadcrumbs**, *or about 1 cup*
5 1/2 tbsp. (80 g) **unsalted butter**
Flour *as needed*
Salt *to taste*

Remove the excess fat from the cutlets or chops, if necessary, and then tenderize the meat with a meat mallet, pounding each cutlet to a thickness of about 1/4 inch (6 mm). Pour the flour onto one plate and the breadcrumbs on another; beat the eggs in a bowl. Flour the cutlets or chops, then dip them in egg, and, lastly, cover them with breadcrumbs, pressing lightly with your hands to make sure the breadcrumbs stick to both sides of each. Heat the butter in a skillet over medium, and when it becomes frothy, add the veal and cook for 3 to 4 minutes on each side, taking care to keep the butter from darkening or starting to smoke. Once cooked, set the cutlets on paper towels to drain, salt lightly and serve with a slice of lemon, if you wish.

BEEF FILET
WITH BALSAMIC VINEGAR

Preparation time: 20 minutes   *Cooking time: 10 minutes*   *Difficulty: easy*

4 SERVINGS

1 3/4 lbs. (800 g) **beef filet**
1 1/2 oz. (40 g) **all-purpose flour**, *or about 1/3 cup*
1/4 cup (60 ml) **balsamic vinegar**
2 tbsp. (30 ml) **extra-virgin olive oil**
1/2 cup (100 ml) **beef broth**
Salt and pepper *to taste*

Cut the filet into four 1- to 1 1/2-inch-thick (3-4 cm) slices, depending
on the width of the meat. Season with salt and pepper and then coat
in flour and shake off any excess.
Heat the oil in a frying pan over medium-high to high heat until it shimmers.
Cook the filet on both sides, then remove the fat (but retain the juices) and add
the balsamic vinegar. When the vinegar has evaporated, remove the filet from
the pan, add the broth and reduce until it thickens (it might take 10-15 minutes).
As soon as the sauce is cooked, pour over the filet and serve.

POTATO-CRUSTED
VEAL TENDERLOIN

Preparation time: 20 minutes   *Cooking time: 5-7 minutes*   *Difficulty: easy*

4 SERVINGS

1 lb. (400 g) **yellow potatoes**, such as Yukon Gold, peeled
1 1/3 lbs. (600 g) **veal tenderloin**
2 1/2 tbsp. (35 ml) **extra-virgin olive oil**
1 **sprig fresh thyme**
Salt and pepper to taste

Heat the oven to 390°F (200°C).
Cut the potatoes using a mandoline with a ripple-cut blade, rotating them
90° between one cut and the next to produce potato "grilles" (waffle cuts).
Soak in cold water. Trim the veal tenderloin of its fat and cut it into four
medallions. Heat 2 tablespoons of the olive oil in a skillet with the thyme over
medium-high heat. Remove the thyme, then sear the medallions, quickly
browning them on both sides (about 3 minutes per side). Season with salt and
pepper. Arrange some of the potatoes on a baking sheet lined with parchment
paper. Overlap the medallions, covering with the remaining potatoes. Season
lightly with salt, drizzle with the remaining oil, and bake for 5 to 7 minutes.

VAL PUSTERIA-STYLE GOULASH

Preparation time: 25 minutes   Cooking time: 2 hours 15 minutes
Difficulty: medium

4 SERVINGS

1 3/4 lbs. (800 g) **beef chuck**, cut into 2-inch pieces
5 **onions**, peeled and chopped
3/4 cup plus 1 1/2 tbsp. (200 ml) **red wine**
1 tsp. (5 g) **paprika**
1 oz. (25 g) **all-purpose flour**, or about 1/4 cup
Zest of one lemon
1 sprig **fresh rosemary**
1 **fresh bay leaf**
1 sprig **fresh marjoram**
2 tbsp. (30 ml) **olive oil**
1 oz. (30 g) **tomato paste**
Salt and pepper to taste

Heat the oil in a pan over medium-high heat and sauté the beef and the onions
for a few minutes until lightly browned. In a glass, dissolve the flour and the
paprika in a little lukewarm water and pour over the meat. Add the red wine
and simmer until it evaporates, then add the herbs, the lemon zest and the
tomato paste and mix well. Add at least a cup of water, cover and simmer
gently for at least 2 hours, until the meat is fork tender. If it becomes too dry,
add a little more water. This dish can be served with polenta,
boiled potatoes or flour dumplings.

SARDINIAN CABBAGE ROLLS

Preparation time: 20 minutes   Cooking time: 20 minutes   Difficulty: easy

4 SERVINGS

1 1/3 lbs. (600 g) **ground beef** or ground lean pork
1 **cabbage with large leaves**, preferably savoy
2 tbsp. (30 ml) **extra-virgin olive oil**
3/4 cup plus 1 1/2 tbsp. (200 ml) **dry white wine**
1 clove **garlic**, chopped
5 **fresh sage leaves**, chopped
3 tbsp. (12 g) **fresh parsley**, chopped
Salt and pepper to taste

In a large bowl combine the ground meat, garlic, sage and parsley. Form the mixture into small cylinders about 1 1/4 inches (3 cm) long and 3/4 inch (2 cm) wide. Parboil the cabbage leaves in salted water, and then wrap around the meat. Heat the oil in a pan and sauté the rolls lightly; add the white wine and simmer until it evaporates. Cover the pan and cook until meat is cooked through, adding water as necessary.

MILANESE –STYLE OSSO BUCO

Preparation time: 20 minutes   Cooking time: 1 hour 40 minutes
Difficulty: medium

4 SERVINGS

*4 **bone-in veal shanks**, 14 oz. (300-400 g) each*
*3 1/2 oz. (100 g) **onion**, peeled and thinly sliced*
*3 1/2 oz. (100 g) **unsalted butter***
*1 3/4 oz. (100 g) **all-purpose flour**, or about 4/5 cup*
*1/2 cup (100 ml) **dry white wine***
*1 cup (250 ml) **beef broth***
*1 clove **garlic**, finely chopped*
*1 **bunch fresh parsley**, finely chopped*
*1 **sprig fresh rosemary**, finely chopped*
Zest of 1/2 lemon
***Salt and pepper** to taste*

Season the veal shanks with salt and pepper, then dredge in flour.
In a large pot, melt the butter and brown the veal on both sides.
Remove from the pan and set aside.
In the same pan, soften the onion over low heat. Put the veal back in the pan,
add the white wine and cook until it evaporates. Add the broth, cover, and
simmer gently until the meat is fork tender.
Meanwhile, mix the garlic, parsley, rosemary and lemon zest together in a small
bowl. Sprinkle the herbs over the osso buco just before serving.

POTATO AND VEAL MEATBALLS

Preparation time: 20 minutes   Cooking time: 7-8 minutes   Difficulty: easy

4 SERVINGS

7 oz. (200 g) **ground veal**
1/2 lb. (250 g) **potatoes**
1 large **egg**, beaten
3 1/2 oz. (100 g) **Parmigiano-Reggiano cheese**, *grated, or about 1 cup*
Freshly grated nutmeg *to taste*
Vegetable oil *for frying*
Salt and pepper *to taste*

Boil the potatoes in a large pot of salted water until tender when pierced with a fork, 15 to 20 minutes. Peel and rice the potatoes.

Mix the ground veal with the potatoes. Season with salt and pepper and a bit of nutmeg. Add the Parmigiano-Reggiano and the egg.

Form the meatballs and flatten them slightly. Fry the meatballs in the oil over medium heat, turning them to cook evenly for about 5 to 10 minutes. Transfer to paper towels to drain.

ROMAN-STYLE MEDALLIONS

Preparation time: 20 minutes   Cooking time: 10 minutes   Difficulty: easy

4 SERVINGS

8 **veal top round slices**, *of about 2 to 2 1/2 oz. (60-70 g)*
8 slices **Parma ham**
1/3 cup plus 1 tbsp. (50 g) **flour**
1/2 stick (50 g) **unsalted butter**
2/3 cup (150 ml) **dry white wine**
8 **fresh sage leaves**
Salt and pepper *to taste*

Trim the slices of veal carefully and pound them gently with a meat mallet till they are 1/4 inch (1/2 cm).

Place a slice of Parma ham and a sage leaf on top of each slice of meat and secure with a toothpick (one variation to the traditional recipe is to roll up the saltimbocca). Flour the meat on the side without the ham.

Melt the butter in a skillet until it turns frothy. Add the meat, starting with the ham side. Sauté the meat, season it with salt and pepper and turn it over to complete cooking for a couple of minutes. Remove the fat from the skillet and deglaze with the wine. Simmer until the wine evaporates and, if necessary, dilute the sauce with a few tablespoons of hot water. Serve immediately.

VEAL SCALLOPINE
ALLA PIZZAIOLA

Preparation time: 30 minutes   Cooking time: 10 minutes   Difficulty: easy

4 SERVINGS

1 lb. 2 oz. (500 g) **plum tomatoes**, *diced*
8 **veal cutlets**, *about 2 oz. (60 g) each*
4 tbsp. (60 ml) **extra-virgin olive oil**
4 1/2 tbsp. (40 g) **capers**, *rinsed*
8 slices **sandwich bread** *(optional)*
Flour, *as needed*
Oregano *to taste*
Salt *to taste*

Cut the crusts off the slices of a sandwich loaf and toast them in the oven or on the grill, if you intend to use them as base for the veal.

Trim the veal cutlets and gently pound them out with a mallet. Heat the oil in a pan over medium, add the veal, lightly coated in flour, and fry them briskly on both sides. Season with salt and keep in a warm place.

In the same pan, add the tomatoes and cook over high heat for 5 minutes. Adjust the seasoning, adding a little salt if necessary, as well as a little oregano and the capers. Return the veal to the pan and finish cooking quickly. Optionally, serve on the toasted bread.

VEAL STEW WITH POTATOES

Preparation time: 20 minutes   Cooking time: 45 minutes   Difficulty: easy

4 SERVINGS

1 3/4 lbs. (800 g) **lean veal**, cubed
1 **carrot**, thinly sliced
1 **onion**, thinly sliced
2 3/4 oz. (80 g) **tomato sauce**
7 tbsp. (100 ml) **white wine**
4 **potatoes**, cut into bite-size pieces
3 1/2 tbsp. (50 g) **unsalted butter**
2 tbsp. (30 ml) **extra-virgin olive oil**
Salt and pepper to taste
1/2 cup plus 2 tsp. (60 g) **all-purpose flour**

Heat the butter in a large pot and sauté the carrot and onion.
Lightly flour the meat, add it to the pot and cook for a few minutes.
Add the white wine, the tomato sauce (which you can dilute with a little water,
if you wish), salt and pepper. When the liquid has reduced by half,
add the potatoes. Cover with water and simmer, uncovered,
for 45 to 50 minutes, until the meat and potatoes are tender.

ROAST VEAL SHANK

Preparation time: 20 minutes   Cooking time: 1 hour   Difficulty: easy

4 SERVINGS

2 2/3 lbs. (1.2 kg) **veal shank**
1 3/4 oz. (50 g) **bacon**, *minced*
1/3 oz. (10 g) **fresh rosemary**, *minced*
Extra-virgin olive oil, *as needed*
3 oz. (80 g) **onion**, *diced*
2 oz. (60 g) **carrots**, *diced*
1 1/2 oz. (40 g) **celery**, *diced*
3/4 cup plus 1 1/2 tbsp. (200 ml) **white wine**
1/2 cup (100 g) **crushed tomatoes**
Beef broth, *as needed*
Minced garlic *to taste*
Salt and pepper *to taste*

Trim the excess fat off the veal shank, make deep slits all over the meat and
season with salt and pepper. Mix together the garlic, rosemary and bacon and
insert it into the slits you have made in the meat.
Heat the oven to 350°F (175°C).
Heat the oil in a pot over medium heat and brown the meat. Add the onion,
carrot and celery and cook until tender. Add the white wine and cook until it
evaporates. Add the crushed tomatoes and stir to combine.
Transfer to a baking pan and cook in the oven; add broth if necessary during
cooking. When the meat is fork tender, in about 1 hour, remove from the pot to
rest. Let the sauce simmer; if necessary, thicken with a little cornstarch dissolved
in a spoonful of water.

BEEF TARTARE

Preparation time: 20 minutes   Difficulty: easy

4 SERVINGS

14 oz. (400 g) **beef tenderloin**
3/4 cup plus 1 1/2 tbsp. (200 ml) **extra-virgin olive oil**
2 **salted anchovies**, *rinsed well and minced*
15 **capers in salt**, *rinsed well*
1 tbsp. **chopped fresh parsley**
3 1/2 oz. (100 g) **red onion**, *or about 1 medium, finely chopped*
Juice of 1 lemon, *as needed*
4 large **eggs**
Salt and pepper *to taste*

Finely chop the beef tenderloin with a knife and divide into 4 portions. Separate the eggs, putting each yolk in a small cup (the whites are not used), and season with salt, pepper and lemon juice to taste. Arrange each serving of beef tartare on a plate together with the egg yolk in its cup. Arrange the anchovies, capers, parsley and red onion on the plates. Each person will add these to the beef tartare according to taste. Season to taste with salt, pepper, and extra-virgin olive oil.

Please use caution in consuming raw and lightly cooked eggs due to the slight risk of salmonella or other food-borne illness. The FDA recommends that children, pregnant women, and anyone with a compromised immune system abstain from eating foods that contain uncooked eggs and meats. To reduce this risk, use only fresh, properly refrigerated, clean grade A or AA eggs with intact shells, and avoid contact between the yolks or whites and the shell. For recipes that call for eggs that are raw or undercooked when the dish is served, use shell eggs that have been treated to destroy salmonella, by pasteurization or another approved method.

STUFFED VEAL ROLLS

Preparation time: 40 minutes   Cooking time: 40 minutes   Difficulty: medium

4 SERVINGS

8 slices of veal
3 1/2 oz. (100 g) ground veal
7 tbsp. (100 g) unsalted butter
3/4 oz. (20 g) dried mushrooms
3/4 oz. (20 g) fresh breadcrumbs
soaked in broth
2 tbsp. (10 g) Parmigiano-Reggiano
cheese, grated

1 bunch fresh parsley
5 fresh sage leaves
5 fresh marjoram leaves
1 large egg, beaten
2 tbsp. (10 ml) milk
2 tbsp. (30 ml) extra-virgin olive oil
Beef broth, as needed
Salt and pepper to taste

Soak the mushrooms in lukewarm water for one hour, and then squeeze out the
excess and chop them together with the herbs.
Melt 5 tablespoons of butter in a skillet over medium-high heat and brown
the ground veal. Let cool completely. To make the stuffing, combine
the soaked breadcrumbs, ground veal, the Parmigiano-Reggiano cheese,
the mushrooms and egg in a large bowl with the milk.
Pound the veal slices. Divide the stuffing evenly, placing a portion on top of each
slice of veal. Roll up veal with stuffing and secure each roll with a toothpick.
Fry the meat rolls in 2 tablespoons of oil and the remaining butter. When they
are browned, season with salt and pepper to taste; add a ladle (about 1/2 cup)
of broth and cook, covered, over low heat for 30 to 40 minutes. Serve lukewarm.

BRAISED VEAL

Preparation time: 20 minutes   Cooking time: 1 hour   Difficulty: medium

4 SERVINGS

1 1/3 lbs. (600 g) **veal flank**
1 3/4 oz. (50 g) **unsalted butter**
4 **slices Parma ham**, *chopped*
3 1/2 tbsp. (50 ml) **dry white wine**
1 **carrot**, *diced small*
2 small **onions**, *peeled*
1 **bunch fresh parsley**
4 **celery leaves**
4 **cloves**
Salt and pepper *to taste*
Beef broth, *as needed*

Remove the fat from the ham and use it to lard the veal.
Stick the cloves into the whole onions. Heat the butter in a large pan over high heat and fry the ham and the two whole onions. Fry the mixture well, then add the veal and brown it all over. Add the carrot; make a bundle of the parsley and celery leaves, and add it to the pan, too. Add the white wine to the pan, season with salt and pepper, and cover. Cook the veal over low heat, turning it frequently. If, during cooking, the meat becomes too dry, add a little broth. Cook until the meat is fork tender. Strain vegetables from juices (reserving juices). Cut the veal into thin slices. Pour some of the juices over veal and serve, with the vegetables alongside.

ASTI-STYLE RABBIT

Preparation time: 30 minutes   Cooking time: 50 minutes   Difficulty: medium

4 SERVINGS

3 1/3 lbs. (1.5 kg) **rabbit**, *cut into pieces*
3/4 cup plus 1 1/2 tbsp. (200 ml) **white wine**
3 1/2 tbsp. (50 ml) **extra-virgin olive oil**
2 cloves **garlic**
1 **onion**, *finely chopped*
1 **sprig fresh rosemary**
1 **bunch fresh sage**
1 **fresh bay leaf**
3 **bell peppers** *(of different colors), diced*
Salt and pepper *to taste*

Heat half of the olive oil in a skillet over medium-high heat. Season the rabbit with salt and pepper and brown it in the oil. In another pan, using the remaining oil, sauté the onion, whole cloves of garlic and herbs. Add the rabbit and the white wine and cook until wine evaporates completely. Cover the skillet and cook over medium heat for about 30 minutes (add peppers after 15 minutes of cooking). Make sure that the cooking juices do not evaporate; if necessary, add a little water.

Transfer the rabbit to a serving platter and let the sauce thicken to taste. Serve the rabbit with the sauce when it is very hot. Discard the garlic.

CHICKEN ALLA CACCIATORE

Preparation time: 30 minutes   Cooking time: 30 minutes   Difficulty: easy

4 SERVINGS

2 1/4 lbs. (1 kg) **ripe tomatoes**, seeded
and chopped into small pieces
1 **chicken** (about 4 lbs.), cut into 8
pieces
1/2 cup (100 ml) **extra-virgin olive oil**
3/4 cup plus 1 1/2 tbsp. (200 ml) **white
wine**
1 **onion**, thinly sliced
1 **carrot**, cut into matchsticks

1 stalk **celery**, cut into matchsticks
1 clove **garlic**
1 **fresh bay leaf**
1 **sprig fresh rosemary**
1 **sprig fresh sage**
Flour, as needed
Chicken broth, as needed
Salt and pepper to taste

Season the chicken with salt and pepper and fry lightly in a pan with oil.
Tie rosemary, bay leaves and sage together with kitchen string.
Put a little oil in a second pan. Add the onion, carrot, celery, garlic, and the herb
bundle and cook until golden.
Add the chicken and the wine, and cook until the wine has evaporated. Add the
chopped tomatoes and continue cooking for about 30 minutes, adding enough
broth to end up with a fairly thick sauce. Add more broth if it has evaporated too
much. When cooked, remove the bundle of herbs. Serve the chicken with a
generous amount of sauce.

CHICKEN
WITH MARSALA AND PEPPERS

Preparation time: 30 minutes   Cooking time: 30 minutes   Difficulty: easy

4 SERVINGS

1 **chicken** (about 4 lbs.), *cut into 4 pieces*
1/3 cup plus 1 1/2 tbsp. (100 ml) **extra-virgin olive oil**
8 oz. (250 g) **red bell pepper**, *or about 1 1/2 large, cut into strips*
8 oz. (250 g) **yellow bell pepper**, *or about 1 1/2 large, cut into strips*
3 1/2 oz. (100 g) **onions**, *or about 1 1/2 small, sliced*
3/4 cup plus 1 1/2 tbsp. (200 ml) **Marsala wine**
1 1/4 cups (300 ml) **chicken broth**
Flour, *as needed*
Cornstarch, *as needed*
1 **sprig fresh rosemary**
Salt and pepper *to taste*

Season the chicken with salt and pepper and coat lightly with flour. In a skillet over medium heat, sauté the chicken pieces in two-thirds of the oil. In a separate pan, sauté the onion with the rosemary in the remaining oil. Add the chicken and the Marsala and cook until the wine evaporates. Add the peppers to the pan and let everything finish cooking, occasionally adding broth as needed and seasoning with salt and pepper to taste. If you prefer a thicker sauce, dissolve a pinch of cornstarch in a few drops of water and stir it in at the very end.

CHICKEN AND POTATO SALAD

Preparation time: 15 minutes Cooking time: 45 minutes
Cooling: 30 minutes Difficulty: easy

4 TO 6 SERVINGS

5 oz. (150 g) **boiled potatoes***, cut into wedges*
1 lb. (400 g) **boneless chicken breasts**
7 oz. (200 g) **mixed salad greens**
2/3 cup (150 ml) **balsamic vinegar**
3 1/2 tbsp. (50 ml) **extra-virgin olive oil**
3 **fresh sage leaves***, chopped*
1 **sprig fresh rosemary***, chopped*
Salt and pepper

Measure out 3 tablespoons of the balsamic vinegar and set aside. Put the
remaining vinegar, salt, half of the herbs, and the chicken breasts in a skillet and
cook over medium heat. Cover with water and bring to a boil, then simmer until
chicken is cooked through, about 40 minutes.
Remove chicken from the liquid and let cool. Cut the chicken into strips and
season with the remaining 1/2 tablespoon of olive oil, the remaining herbs and a
sprinkling of freshly ground pepper.
Toss the salad greens with the remaining oil and the reserved balsamic vinegar,
along with a pinch of salt. Arrange the slices of chicken and the potatoes on a
bed of greens and serve.

TURKEY WITH TRUFFLES

Preparation time: 45 minutes   Cooking time: 45 minutes   Difficulty: medium

4 SERVINGS

1 1/3 lbs. (600 g) **boneless turkey breast**
5 tbsp. (75 ml) **heavy cream**
1 large **egg white**
1 **black truffle**, weighing approximately 1 oz. (30 g)
Fresh rosemary to taste
5 tsp. (25 ml) **extra-virgin olive oil**
Salt and pepper to taste

Cut the turkey breast lengthwise, butterfly it and pound it well to make it tender. Trim the meat and, with the pieces you cut off (about 5 1/4 oz. [150 g]), prepare the filling. In a food processor fitted with the blade attachment, pulse until the meat is finely minced. Transfer to a large bowl and add the egg white, cream, and salt and pepper, and stir the filling well to combine.

Clean the truffle, dice it into 1/12-inch (2 mm) cubes and mix it in with the rest of the filling. Season the turkey breast with salt and pepper, spread the filling over it and roll it up. Secure the roll with kitchen twine.

Heat the oil in a pan over medium heat and sear all sides of the turkey. Reduce heat, add the rosemary and cook for another 30 minutes, uncovered, adding a few tablespoons of water if necessary. Let the turkey roll cool before slicing it. Strain the cooking juices with a fine-mesh sieve; discard solids. Serve with the cooking juices and a few truffle shavings to taste.

ROASTED TURKEY BREAST

Preparation time: 20 minutes   Cooking time: 1 hour 15 minutes
Difficulty: medium

4 SERVINGS

1 3/4 lbs. (800 g) **boneless turkey breast**
1 lb. (450 g) **broccoli**, *cut into florets*
7 oz. (200 g) **hazelnuts**, *or about 1 3/4 cups*
3 1/2 oz. (100 g) **onions**, *or about 1 1/2 small, diced*
2 3/4 oz. (80 g) **carrots**, *or about 1 1/2 small, diced*
2 oz. (60 g) **celery**, *or about 3 1/2 small stalks, diced*

1/3 cup plus 1 1/2 tbsp. (100 ml) **white wine**
Chicken broth, *as needed*
Cornstarch, *as needed*
2 cloves **garlic**
Fresh sage *to taste*
Fresh rosemary *to taste*
Fresh bay leaves *to taste*
1/3 cup (80 ml) **extra-virgin olive oil**
Salt and pepper *to taste*

Heat the oven to 350°F (175°C). Sear the turkey in a pan with half the oil. Season it generously with salt and pepper. Add the onion, carrot and celery to the pan with a whole clove garlic and the herbs. Cook for a few minutes. Add the wine and cook until it evaporates. Then roast in the oven, adding a bit of broth occasionally, if necessary, until the turkey's internal temperature reaches 165°F (75°C), about 1 hour When the meat is done, remove the garlic and herbs and strain the drippings. If necessary, add some cornstarch dissolved in a bit of water to thicken the drippings into a gravy. Add the hazelnuts (toasted in a nonstick pan and roughly chopped) and let the meat absorb the flavors for a few minutes. Bring a pan of lightly salted water to a boil and cook the broccoli for 10 minutes. Heat the remaining oil in a par with the other garlic clove. Strain the broccoli and add it to the pan. Let it cook for 5 minutes, crushing it with a spoon. Season it with salt and pepper to taste. Slice the turkey breast and top it with the gravy. Serve it with crushed broccoli on the side.

CHICKEN STUFFED
WITH CHESTNUTS

Preparation time: 1 hour   Cooking time: 1 hour 15 minutes   Difficulty: high

4 SERVINGS

1 **chicken**, about 2 lbs (1 kg)
14 oz. (400 g) **sausage**, casing removed
3 1/2 oz. (100 g) **chestnuts**
1 large **egg**
7 oz. (200 g) **onion**, diced
5 1/3 oz. (150 g) **carrots**, diced
2 1/2 oz. (80 g) **celery**, diced

2 cloves **garlic**, peeled
5 tsp. (25 ml) **extra-virgin olive oil**
Fresh **rosemary, thyme, bay leaf** and
sage to taste
Nutmeg to taste
Salt and pepper to taste

Heat the oven to 360°F (180°C).
Bone the chicken breast by removing the breastbone, and season the inside with
salt and pepper. To prepare the stuffing, mix the sausage meat with the egg and
a pinch of nutmeg. Season with salt and pepper to taste.
Boil the chestnuts and let them cool before peeling them, taking care not to
break them, and add them to the stuffing. Stuff the chicken with the filling and
close the breast opening using a kitchen needle and twine.
Sauté the chicken in a roasting pan with the olive oil, then add the carrot, onion,
celery, the herbs and the whole cloves of garlic, and roast in the oven for 50
minutes to an hour. If necessary, add a little water to prevent meat from drying out.
As soon as the chicken is cooked, wrap it in parchment paper and put it aside.
Deglaze and filter the cooking juices (you can make a gravy from the juices, if
desired). Slice the chicken and serve it with the gravy.

GUINEA FOWL
IN PEVERADA SAUCE

Preparation time: 30 minutes   Cooking time: 45 minutes   Difficulty: medium

4 SERVINGS

FOR THE GUINEA FOWL
1 **guinea fowl**, about 2 1/4 lbs. (1 kg)
7 oz. (200 g) **bacon**, diced
1 clove **garlic**, peeled
2 tbsp. (30 ml) **extra-virgin olive oil**
1/3 cup plus 1 1/2 tbsp. (100 ml) **white wine**
Fresh sage and rosemary to taste
Salt and pepper to taste

FOR THE SAUCE
1 3/4 oz. (50 g) **soppressa vicentina** (Vicenza salami), chopped (or dry Italian salami)
1 **guinea fowl liver**
2 tbsp. **fresh parsley**, chopped
Zest of 1 lemon
2 **salt-packed anchovies**, rinsed well
2 tbsp. (30 ml) **extra-virgin olive oil**
2 tbsp. (30 ml) **vinegar**
Salt and pepper to taste

Clean the guinea fowl thoroughly, keeping the liver to one side.
Season the bird with salt and pepper inside and outside and sauté in a saucepan in the oil with the bacon, garlic and a few sprigs of sage and rosemary.
Add the white wine and cook until the wine evaporates. Continue to cook over low heat, uncovered, for about 45 minutes, adding a few tablespoons of lukewarm water from time to time. When cooked, divide the guinea fowl into pieces and keep warm. Skim fat from the cooking juices; filter the juices through a sieve and set aside. Meanwhile, mix the anchovies, the guinea fowl liver and the salami and sauté in a small skillet with the oil. Add the vinegar and cook until it evaporates. Then add the parsley, lemon zest, the cooking juices from the guinea fowl and a generous sprinkling of pepper. Reduce the sauce.
Serve the guinea fowl with the Peverada Sauce.

GUINEA FOWL
WITH CABBAGE AND PORCINI MUSHROOMS

Preparation time: 20 minutes   Cooking time: 50 minutes   Difficulty: medium

4 SERVINGS

2 lbs. 3 oz. (1 kg) **guinea fowl breast**
1/2 lb. **cabbage,** *roughly chopped*
1/3 lb. **porcini mushrooms,** *cleaned and diced*
1/2 cup **white wine**
1 sprig **rosemary**
2 cloves **garlic**
1/4 cup **extra-virgin olive oil,** *plus more for drizzling*
1 tbsp. **minced parsely**
Salt and pepper *to taste*

Heat the oven to 350°F (175°C).

Clean and rinse the guinea fowl. Season the outside with salt and 2 tablespoons oil and the inside with rosemary and garlic. Place in a roasting pan and roast for about 30 minutes. Clean the cabbage and blanch in salted water for 3 to 4 minutes. Drain, reserving the water.

Mince the rosemary. Sauté the mushrooms in 2 tablespoons of oil with the garlic clove and rosemary. Add the cabbage to the mushrooms.

Season with salt and pepper and cook a few minutes.

Pour in some of the cooking water from the cabbage.

When the guinea fowl is removed from the oven, divide it into 8 pieces. Transfer the pieces to the pan of vegetables and stew for about 20 minutes. Sprinkle each serving with pepper and a drizzle of olive oil.

DUCK BREAST WITH HONEY

Preparation time: 20 minutes   Cooking time: 15 minutes   Difficulty: medium

4 SERVINGS

*2 **duck breasts***
*1 3/4 oz. (50 g) **onion**, sliced*
*1 clove **garlic**, peeled*
*3 tbsp. (approx. 60 g) **honey***
***Fresh rosemary, sage and bay leaf** to taste*
***Salt and pepper** to taste*

With a sharp knife make slits in the skin of the duck breasts, being careful not to cut the meat. Season the duck breasts with salt and pepper and sauté them in a skillet, skin side down, until most of the fat is rendered and the skin is lightly golden. Flip the duck breasts over and cook for a few minutes
Transfer the duck breasts to a baking pan, skin side up, then add the garlic, the onion and the herbs. Bake for about 10 minutes, leaving the duck soft and pink inside. Let duck rest for a few minutes, loosely wrapped in aluminum foil, before slicing. Remove the cooking fat from the baking pan and then add the honey. When you have obtained the desired thickness, filter the sauce through a sieve. Serve the duck breasts covered with the honey sauce.

GRILLED LAMB RIBS

Preparation time: 20 minutes   Cooking time: 10 minutes   Difficulty: easy

4 SERVINGS

1 1/3 lbs. (600 g) **lamb rib chops**
3 1/2 tbsp. (50 ml) **extra-virgin olive oil**
Chopped fresh thyme *to taste*
Chopped fresh rosemary *to taste*
Salt and pepper *to taste*

Heat the grill to medium-high.

Trim the excess fat from the chops if necessary. Pound them lightly with a mallet then marinate for 10 minutes with the olive oil, thyme and rosemary.

Cook the lamb chops on the grill for 4 to 5 minutes on each side. Season them with salt and pepper and serve immediately, while they are still piping hot, with a side dish of your choice.

LAMB, PARMA HAM AND EGGS

Preparation time: 30 minutes   Cooking time: 1 hour   Difficulty: medium

4 SERVINGS

2 1/4 lbs. (1 kg) **lamb**, *cut into chunks*
3 1/2 oz. (100 g) **Parma ham**, *thinly sliced*
1 cup (250 ml) **dry white wine**
1 oz. (25 g) **lard**
1/2 cup (100 ml) **beef broth**
1 **onion**, *thinly sliced*
All–purpose flour, *as needed*
Grated nutmeg *to taste*
3 **large egg yolks**, *beaten*
Juice of 1/2 lemon
Salt and pepper *to taste*

Heat the oven to 350°F (175°C).
Put the lard, the ham and the onion in a large pan. Gently fry over medium heat.
Add salt, pepper and a pinch of nutmeg to taste.
Coat the lamb lightly in flour, add to the pan and sauté. Pour in the broth and
reduce by half. Add the white wine, salt and pepper and cook over low heat until
the lamb is fork tender.
Arrange lamb on a hot serving plate. Pour the juices from the meat into a small
pan and blend in the egg yolks together with the lemon juice. Mix and leave
over low heat for a minute, then pour the sauce over the meat. Bake until a
golden crust forms. Serve immediately.

ROASTED LAMB SKEWERS

Preparation time: 50 minutes   Cooking time: 10 minutes   Difficulty: easy

4 SERVINGS

1 3/4 lbs. (800 g) **lamb**, cut into 1/3-3/4-inch (1-2 cm) cubes
2 1/2 lbs. (1.2 kg) **potatoes**, or about 3 1/2 large, peeled and cut into wedges
2 cloves **garlic**
2 sprigs **fresh thyme**
1 oz. (30 g) **fresh rosemary**
2/3 cup (150 ml) **extra-virgin olive oil**
Salt and pepper to taste

Heat the oven to 350°F (175°C).
Slide the lamb onto skewers.
Preheat a baking dish. Parboil the potatoes in salted water for 5 minutes, drain, and place them in the preheated baking dish with half the oil, 1 garlic clove, salt and pepper. Bake for 30 minutes.
Strip the thyme leaves from the stem and thinly slice the other garlic clove. Spread them over the skewers and drizzle the remaining olive oil over top. Let the meat marinate for at least 20 to 30 minutes in the refrigerator. To keep the garlic and thyme from burning, remove them from the meat before grilling. Let the skewers warm up to room temperature for about 10 minutes. Cook them on a grill or flat griddle for about 10 minutes, seasoning with salt and pepper to taste.

LEG OF LAMB COOKED IN HAY

Preparation time: 20 minutes   Cooking time: 4 hours   Difficulty: medium

4 SERVINGS

5 1/2 lbs. (2.5 kg) **leg of lamb**
3 1/2 tbsp. (50 ml) **extra-virgin olive oil**
2 cloves **garlic**, *peeled*
Fresh bay leaf, thyme and rosemary chopped *to taste*
Hay, *as needed (clean eating hay, not bedding hay; a few handfuls of hay should do*
Salt and pepper *to taste*

Bone the leg of lamb, spread salt and pepper on the inside and cover it with half of the chopped herbs (bay leaf, thyme and rosemary) and a clove of garlic. Put the leg back together again and tie it with kitchen twine.

Spread salt and pepper on the outside of the leg and fry it in an ovenproof skillet with the olive oil and the remaining herbs until browned. Transfer to the oven and roast at 360°F (180°C) for about 1 hour.

Remove the lamb from the oven and dilute the cooking juices with a ladleful of water. Filter the liquid and set it aside.

Envelop the cooked leg in hay, wrap it all in a paper oven bag and return it to the oven to roast at 210°F (100°C) for about 3 hours. Remove the lamb from the oven bag and slice. Serve together with the cooking juices.

TUSCAN-STYLE
ROAST LOIN OF PORK

Preparation time: 30 minutes   Cooking time: 1 hour 15 minutes
Difficulty: easy

4 SERVINGS

2 1/4 lbs. (1 kg) **bone-in pork loin roast**
2 cloves **garlic**, *chopped*
2 sprigs **fresh rosemary**, *chopped*
7 tbsp. (100 ml) **extra-virgin olive oil**
Salt and pepper *to taste*

Heat the oven to 350°F (175°C).
Partially separate the bones from the joint of meat without removing the bone.
Mix together the garlic, rosemary, a generous pinch of salt and a pinch of
pepper. Distribute half of the mixture between the bone and the meat. Tie the
two parts of the joint together with kitchen twine. Distribute the rest of the garlic
and rosemary mixture over the outside of the meat, massaging well.
Place the meat in a roasting pan. Drizzle with oil and roast in the oven for about
1 hour, or until a meat thermometer inserted into center of pork reads 155°F
(68°C). Let rest for 10 minutes, remove the twine and the bone and slice the
meat. Serve with the warm cooking juices.

PORK FILET WITH HAM

Preparation time: 20 minutes *Cooking time: 20 minutes* *Difficulty: easy*

4 SERVINGS

2 **pork filets**, *about 1 2/3 lb. (750 g)*
12 **slices Parma ham**
Balsamic vinegar, *preferably balsamic of Modena, to taste*
1 **sprig fresh rosemary**
2 cloves **garlic**
10 1/2 oz. (300 g) **baby salad greens**
Extra-virgin olive oil, *as needed*
Salt and pepper *to taste*

Remove the excess fat from the slices of ham.
Cut the pork filets into small pieces, about 2 oz. (60 g) each. Wrap each piece of pork in a slice of ham, fixing it in place with a toothpick.
Heat a little olive oil in a frying pan and add the rosemary, the garlic and the pieces of pork. Drizzle the meat with the balsamic vinegar. Cook the meat on both sides until the center is no longer pink.
Before serving, place the meat on a bed of baby greens and season with salt, freshly ground black pepper and olive oil. Pour the reduced balsamic vinegar sauce over the top.

CASSOEULA PORK
AND CABBAGE STEW

Preparation time: 20 minutes   Cooking time: 2 hours Difficulty: medium

4 SERVINGS

2 lbs. (900 g) **pork spareribs**
1 3/4 lbs. (800 g) **fresh pork sausage**
1 3/4 lbs. (800 g) **savoy cabbage***, sliced*
7 oz. (200 g) **onion***, sliced*
3 1/2 tbsp. (50 ml) **extra-virgin olive oil**
1 2/3 cups (400 g) **crushed tomatoes**
Chopped fresh sage and rosemary *to taste*
Salt and pepper *to taste*

To facilitate cooking and prevent the meat from drying, you can parboil the pork
ribs and sausages (separately) in boiling salted water for 30 minutes.
Meanwhile, sauté the onion in a large skillet with the olive oil.
Add the cabbage and cook for a few minutes. Add the crushed tomatoes,
season with salt and pepper, and then add the meat.
Cook over low heat for about 2 hours. When the meat is cooked, add the herbs.

PORK SPARERIBS WITH POLENTA

Preparation time: 20 minutes   Cooking time: 1 hour   Difficulty: medium

4 SERVINGS

2 1/4 lbs. (1 kg) **slightly smoked pork spare ribs,**
cut into 2-2 1/2-inch (5-6 cm) **chunks**
1 3/4 oz. (50 g) **unsalted butter**
2 1/2 cups (5 ml) **white wine**
Salt and pepper *to taste*

FOR THE POLENTA
2 cups plus 2 tsp (500 ml) **water**
3 1/2 oz. (100 g) **cornmeal**

Cook the spare ribs in an earthenware saucepan with the butter, salt and pepper for 30 minutes. Add the white wine and continue cooking over low heat until the ribs are tender. Meanwhile pour the water into a saucepan, bring to a boil and add salt. Pour in the cornmeal in a steady stream stirring with a whisk at the same time. Cook for about 30 minutes stirring from time to time with a wooden spoon

PORK TENDERLOIN
IN MARSALA WINE

Preparation time: 30 minutes   Cooking time: 15 minutes   Difficulty: medium

4 SERVINGS

17 1/2 oz. (500 g) **pork tenderloin**
3 1/2 oz. (100 g) **caul fat**
1 3/4 oz. (50 g) **lard or bacon**, finely
chopped
1/2 clove **garlic**, finely chopped
2 1/4 tbsp. (30 ml) **extra-virgin olive oil**
3 1/2 tbsp. (50 g) **unsalted butter**
1/3 cup plus 1 1/2 tbsp. (100 ml)
Marsala wine

1 3/4 oz. (50 g) **Parma ham**, sliced
Chopped fresh sage to taste
Chopped fresh rosemary to taste
Chopped fresh thyme to taste
All-purpose flour, as needed
Salt and pepper to taste

Heat the oven to 390°F (200 °C).
Rinse the caul fat under running water.
Prepare a mixture of lard or bacon, sage, rosemary, thyme and garlic.
Trim any excess fat from the pork tenderloin, season with salt and pepper and
spread the lard–herb mixture over it. Wrap it in the Parma ham and then in the
caul fat. Flour the pork lightly and sauté in a skillet with the oil and butter, then
add the bits of meat that you have trimmed off. Place in a roasting pan and roast
in the oven for 12 to 13 minutes, or until a meat thermometer inserted into
center of pork reads 155°F (68°C).
Remove the pork from the roasting pan and keep warm. Remove the excess fat,
deglaze the baking pan with Marsala wine, and reduce the cooking juices as
much as necessary. Slice the meat and serve with the sauce.

EGGPLANT PARMIGIANA

Preparation time: 30 minutes   Cooking time: 1 hour   Difficulty: medium

4 SERVINGS

*1 lb. (500 g) **eggplant**, thinly sliced*
*2 3/4 oz. (80 g) **all-purpose flour**, or about 4/5 cup*
*2 large **eggs**, beaten*
*10 1/2 oz. (300 g) **tomato sauce***
*3 1/2 oz. (100 g) **mozzarella cheese**, crumbled*
*3 1/2 oz. (100 g) **Parmigiano-Reggiano cheese**, grated, or about 1 cup*
*3 1/2 oz. (100 g) **fresh pork sausages**, casing removed and crumbled*
*2 tbsp. (30 ml) **extra-virgin olive oil***
***Vegetable oil**, as needed*
***Salt** to taste*

Slice the eggplant, then put it in a colander, salt it lightly and allow it to drain for about 30 minutes. Heat the oven to 350°F (175°C). Dredge the eggplant slices in flour and then dip in the egg. Heat the vegetable oil in a skillet until hot and shimmering. Fry the eggplant until golden brown on both sides. Transfer to a plate lined with paper towels to drain. Pour a thin layer of tomato sauce over the bottom of a 9-by-13-inch baking dish, then arrange a layer of eggplant slices. Cover with mozzarella and sausage, then some tomato sauce and sprinkle with Parmigiano-Reggiano. Add another layer of eggplant, repeating the layering of ingredients until all but a small amount of sauce and Parmigiano are used (the last layer must be of eggplant slices). Top with sauce and Parmigiano-Reggiano cheese, then bake in the oven until the top has formed a golden crust.

Note: You can substitute zucchini for the eggplant if you wish. The preparation is the same, but the zucchini must be sliced lengthwise. You can also replace the sausage with a layer of sliced Mortadella.

INGREDIENTS INDEX

PHOTO CREDITS

All photographs are by ACADEMIA BARILLA except the following:
pages 6, 95 ©123RF

The Taunton Press
Inspiration for hands-on living®

The Taunton Press, Inc.
63 South Main Street
PO Box 5506, Newtown, CT 06470-5506
e-mail: tp@taunton.com

Translations:
Catherine Howard - Mary Doyle - John Venerella - Free z'be, Paris
Salvatore Ciolfi - Rosetta Translations SARL

LIBRARY OF CONGRESS CATALOGING-IN-PUBLICATION DATA IN PROGRESS
ISBN: 978-1-62710-048-9

Printed in China
10 9 8 7 6 5 4 3 2 1